Dear Daughter

Dear Daughter

A Book of Love, Hope, and Wisdom
to Last a Lifetime

Wendy L. Gardner

spruce

An Hachette UK Company
First published in Great Britain in 2010 by Spruce
a division of Octopus Publishing Group Ltd
Endeavour House, 189 Shaftesbury Avenue, London, WC2H 8JG
www.octopusbooks.co.uk
www.octopusbooksusa.com

Distributed in the U.S. and Canada for Octopus Books USA
c/- Hachette Book Group USA
237 Park Avenue
New York NY 10017.

Copyright ©2010 Hollan Publishing Inc.
Illustrations ©2010 Robert D. Bretz
Design by Wendy Simard

Wendy L. Gardner asserts the moral right to be identified as the author
of this book.

ISBN 13 978-1-84601-357-7
ISBN 10 1-84601-357-7

A CIP catalog record for this book is available from the Library of Congress.

Printed and bound in China

10 9 8 7 6 5 4 3 2 1

To Willa, the greatest gift of my life.

Contents

Only parents' love
can last our lives.

—Robert Browning

Introduction

Whether you are the parent of a newborn, preschooler, preteen, adolescent or a grown adult, there is nothing that equals the profound love you feel for this life that you've brought into the world. Parenting can be like a never-ending roller coaster ride—exciting but overwhelming, exhilarating but scary, and a delightful but nauseating experience all wrapped up in one. When you're ensconced in the day-to-day trenches of work, parenthood, marriage, and various other commitments, it can be challenging to find time to share special memories and aspirations from your own life with your child. **Dear Daughter** is an opportunity to communicate your hopes and dreams, track special milestones, and pass along beliefs and values to your daughter.

The purpose of this book is to help you leave a lasting written legacy that articulates the deep, unconditional love that you will always have for your daughter. Without the daunting impact of a blank journal to fill, you will be able to easily organize your thoughts and express them without intimidation. This journal is appropriate for either a mother or father to write in. Parents can fill it out with each other, or each parent can respond on his or her own. If you have more than one daughter, you should complete a separate journal for each one. **Dear Daughter** works for children of any age, at any stage of life, so you can write in it when your daughter is little, and then again on her graduation, wedding day, or the birth of her first child.

This journal will help build your daughter's self-awareness, informing her decisions and sense of self, helping her to flourish and shape who she will become. **Dear Daughter** will be a memento to which she can refer during each different stage of her life, to be continually reminded of your infinite love and guidance.

insert photo of you and your daughter here

Memory is the diary that we all carry about with us.

—Oscar Wilde

Chapter One: My Life

Self Portrait

My given name: ....

Name I like to be called: ....

Date and place of birth: ....

My ethnic heritage: ....

Current age: ....

Eye color: ....

Hair color: ....

My astrological sign: ....

The Early Years

insert photo of you as a child

I had .... siblings growing up.

In regard to birth order, I was: ....

Having siblings is: ....

....

....

....

Not having siblings is: ....

....

....

....

I grew up in a: _____

Growing up in that sort of environment taught me: _____

_____

_____

_____

_____

My best friend from childhood was: _____

If you asked my friends or family to describe me as a child in one

word, it would be: _____

I shared a bedroom with my: _____

By sharing a bedroom, I learned: _____

_____

When I was a kid, I loved to pretend: _____

_____

My favorite food growing up was: _____

_____

A special dish that my _____ made growing up was:

_____

I learned to swim at age: ....

I learned to ride a bike at age: ....

The first time that I rode a horse I remember: ....

....

....

What I loved most about ice skating was: ....

....

....

What I loved most about roller skating was: ....

....

....

The household chores I was responsible for as a child were:

....

....

I typically spent my allowance on: ....

....

....

My favorite candy was: ....

....

My favorite outfit or garment that I wore often was: ....
....

While growing up, I collected: ....

My best birthday ever was: ....

....

....

My favorite season growing up was: ....

One of my favorite memories of a seasonal outing I took with my

family at this time of year was: ....

....

....

....

....

....

My best holiday memory was: ....

....

....

....

....

Some active pursuits that my family enjoyed together were:

....

....

I had .... pet(s) growing up.

My pet's name(s) was / were: ....

Having a pet(s) taught me: ....

....

....

The game / toy I couldn't live without was: ....

....

The grandparent I was closest to was: ....

....

A memorable outing with this grandparent was: ....

....

....

....

My favorite aunt or uncle was: ....

....

The cousin(s) with whom I spent time growing up was / were:

....

One of favorite memories with my cousin(s) was: ....

....

....

....

....

School was something I always liked / disliked (circle one) because:

....

....

....

For elementary school, I went to: ....

....

My favorite subject was: ....

For lunch, I usually had: ....

My favorite after-school snack was: ....

....

My favorite elementary school teacher was: ....

....

For middle school, I went to: ....

My favorite middle school teacher was: ....

....

The sports I played were: ....

....

....

The musical instrument I played was: ....

....

Other extracurricular activities I did: ....

....

....

....

My favorite memory from summer camp is: ....

....

....

....

My favorite Halloween costume was: ....

....

....

My favorite book growing up was: ....
....

My favorite TV show was: ....
....

In regard to religion, my family: ....
....
....
....

I always wanted to be ....when I grew up.

Something I used to get disciplined for when I was young was:
....
....
....

My father's job was: ....
....
....

My mother's job was: ....
....
....

My mother would occasionally devote a day specifically to me. One of my fondest memories of one of those days is: ....

....

....

....

....

....

....

....

My father would occasionally devote a day specifically to me. One of my fondest memories of one of those days is: ....

....

....

....

....

....

....

....

My Teenage Years

insert photo of you as a teenager

For high school, I went to:

It was located:

In regard to grades, I received mostly:

My favorite subject in high school was:

My least favorite subject in high school was:

My favorite teacher in high school was:

The sports I played in high school were: ....
....

The plays and musicals in which I appeared in high school were:

....

....

....

Other extracurricular activities in which I was involved were:

....

....

....

The people who sat at my lunch table were: ....

....

....

My best friends were: ....

....

The type of music I listened to was: ....

....

The first concert that I ever attended was: ....

....

My first romantic crush was: ....

I was ....years old when I had my first date.

My first kiss was: ....

In regard to dating, my parents were: ....

....

....

....

My mother influenced my attitudes toward relationships by:

....

....

....

....

....

My father influenced my attitudes toward relationships by:

....

....

....

....

....

The most memorable thing about attending my high school's home-coming was: ....

....

The most memorable thing about attending my high school prom was:

....

....

....

Popularity in high school is: ....

....

Most of the time I wore: ....

....

My favorite celebrity or teen idol was: ....

Talking on the phone in high school was: ....

....

My favorite TV show was: ....

....

A popular movie that I loved during my teen years was:

....

....

In regard to physical maturation, I was: ....

....

I felt insecure about: ....

....

....

In regard to discipline / behavior, I was: ....

....

....

....

My job during high school was: ....

....

I was .... years old when I got my driver's license.

The most memorable thing about learning to drive was: ....

....

....

....

The car that I drove was: ....

I liked / disliked (circle one) that car because: ....

....

When I was a teenager, I felt pressure regarding: ....

....

....

....

....

The most challenging situation that I dealt with when I was a

teenager was: ....

....

....

....

....

....was always a source of encouragement to me.

The most important piece of advice that was offered to me when I

was a teen was: ....

....

....

....

....

....

....

My Young Adult Years

insert photo of you as a young adult

After high school, I: ....

....

The highest academic level I achieved is: ....

The first time that I was out on my own, I remember: ....

....

....

....

The best roommate that I ever had was: ....

The worst roommate that I ever had was: ....

In regard to the school of hard knocks, I've experienced:

....

....

....

....

When I was a young adult, I got my first: ....

....

My first "real" job was: ....

A mentor to me in my young adult years was: ....

....

The best piece of advice I ever received during these years was:

....

....

....

....

....

....

....

....

All Grown Up

insert photo of you as an adult

Two adjectives that describe me today are:

....

A cause that I feel strongly about is:

....

....

To me, religion is:

....

....

I consider myself a spiritual person because:

....

............................influences me now, as an adult, because

....

My favorite place that I have lived is: ....

....

The place where I feel most peaceful is: ....

....

My favorite book is: ....

....

My favorite author is: ....

My favorite poem is: ....

My favorite poet is: ....

My favorite movie is: ....

My favorite actor / actress is: ....

....

My favorite artist is: ....

My favorite painting / sculpture / artwork is: ....

....

My favorite meal is: ....

My favorite dessert is: ....

My favorite time of day is: ....

My favorite season is: ....

My favorite holiday is: ....

....

My favorite word is: ....

My favorite song is: ....

My favorite musical artist is: ....

....

My favorite color is: ....

My favorite sport to watch is: ....

My favorite sport to play is: ....

I enjoy traveling with: ....

....

My career is: ....

I met my spouse: ....

....

I knew that my spouse was "the one" when: ....

....

....

My favorite thing about my spouse when I met him / her was:

....

....

My favorite thing about my spouse today is: ....

....

....

My wedding date: ....

Ceremony location: ....

Reception location: ....

Wedding party: ....

Best man: ....

Maid of honor: ....

.... gave the funniest toast.

.... gave the most sentimental toast.

For our honeymoon, we:..
....

The most important thing about relationships that I've learned from

my spouse:..
....
....
....

The most difficult decision I've ever had to make as an adult was:

....
....
....
....

People who inspire me are:..
....
....
....
....

My clearest memory of my mother is:

....

....

....

....

....

My clearest memory of my father is:

....

....

....

....

....

Some of the dreams / goals that I have fulfilled in my life are:

....

....

....

....

....

....

....

....

One thing that I would like to change about myself is:

....

....

....

One thing that I hope to **never** change about myself is:

....

....

....

If I could erase one thing I've done in my life, it would be:

....

....

....

The person closest to me whom I've lost was: ....

....

The top 5 things in my life for which I'm grateful are:

1. ....

2. ....

3. ....

4. ....

5. ....

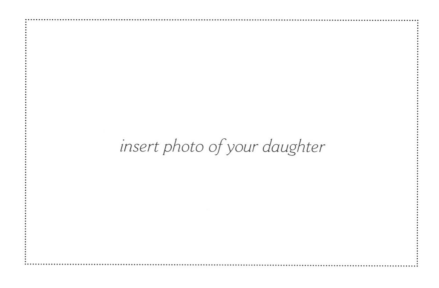

insert photo of your daughter

Making the decision to have
a child—it's momentous.
It is to decide forever to have
your heart go walking around
outside your body.

—Elizabeth Stone

Chapter Two: My Daughter

When I found out that I was going to be a parent, I felt:

....

....

....

....

....

....

....

....

....

....

....

....

Date you were born: ....

City, State: ....

Hospital: ....

Doctor who delivered you: ....

Time: ....

Height: ....

Weight: ....

Eye color: ....

Hair color: ....

People thought you looked like: ....

On the day you were born, I remember: ....

....

....

....

When I learned that I had a baby girl: ....

....

The first time I looked into your eyes and held you, I thought:

....

....

....

....

....

....

....

....

This is why I named you: ....

....

....

A nickname I often called you was: ....

....

....

The first house or apartment that you lived in was: ....

....

....

....

The first time that you. . .

Slept through the night: ....

Smiled: ....

Laughed out loud: ....

Rolled over: ....

Sat up alone: ....

Crawled: ....

Bathed in the tub: ....

Waved bye-bye: ....

Ate solids: ....

Drank from a cup: ....

Stood up on your own: ....

Took your first steps: ....

Danced: ....

Dressed yourself: ....

Used the potty: ....

Drew a picture: ....

Got your first haircut: ....

Wrote your name: ....

Your first word was ...., and the context in which you said it was

....

You reminded me of .... when you were a toddler.

My favorite outfit I dressed you in as a little girl was:

....

When you were a tiny baby, you used to love gazing at:

....

....

One word that would describe you as a toddler: ....

Your favorite book as a child was: ....

....

Your favorite food as a child was: ....

Your favorite doll as a child was: ....

Watching you play: ....

....

....

....

....

Hearing you giggle: ....

....

....

....

....

Seeing you dance: ....

....

....

....

....

Seeing you discover: ....

....

....

....

We never left home without your: ....

You made me laugh when: ....

....

....

....

....

The ways in which you were extremely "girly" were: ....

....

....

....

....

The ways in which you were a "tomboy" were: ....

....

....

....

....

Your baby talk made me: ....

....

....

....

Watching you explore:

....

....

....

....

A routine that we consistently shared was:

....

....

....

I nurtured your independence by:

....

....

....

....

Learning to share was:

....

....

....

....

Proper manners and etiquette are important to learn because:

....

....

....

....

....

Swearing is inappropriate because: ....

....

....

....

Being a parent allows me to see my parents in a different light because:

....

....

....

....

....

....

....

....

My mother taught me this about parenting:

_____

_____

_____

_____

_____

_____

_____

My father taught me this about parenting:

_____

_____

_____

_____

_____

_____

_____

_____

The things my mother did that I hope to repeat with you are:

....

....

....

....

....

....

....

....

....

The things my mother did that I hope **not** to repeat with you are:

....

....

....

....

....

....

....

....

....

The things my father did that I hope to repeat with you are:

....

....

....

....

....

....

....

....

The things my father did that I hope **not** to repeat with you are:

....

....

....

....

....

....

....

....

....

Some things my grandparents taught me about parenting are:

....

....

....

....

....

One of my favorite things to do with you on a daily basis is:

....

....

....

One of the fondest memories I have shared with you is:

....

....

....

....

....

....

....

....

....

....

You look most adorable when you:

....

....

....

Parenting has changed me as a person because:

....

....

....

....

....

....

....

You bring joy to me every day because:

....

....

....

....

....

....

Qualities of myself that I see in you are:

....

....

....

....

....

....

Being with you enables me to be present in my life today because:

....

....

....

....

....

....

My favorite vacation that I have ever taken with you is:

....

....

....

....

....

I am proud of you for:

....

....

....

....

....

....

Once upon a time you:

....

....

....

....

....

....

You displayed leadership qualities when:

....

....

....

....

....

....

It's important to me to teach you about nature because:

....

....

....

....

....

....

I realized that you were becoming your own person when:

....

....

....

....

....

....

....

I'll never forget when you: ....

....

....

....

....

What it means to me to be a parent:

I would like to include these aspects of my childhood in yours:

If you have a daughter of your own, I hope:

....

....

....

....

....

....

....

....

....

Parent–daughter relationships are particularly special because:

....

....

....

....

....

....

....

....

....

The things I love most about you are:

You bring a sense of purpose to my life because:

The most important thing that you have taught me about myself is:

....

....

....

....

....

....

....

....

When I look at you today, I think: ....

....

....

....

....

....

....

....

There are two lasting
bequests we can give
our children.
One is roots.
The other is wings.

—Hodding Carter

Chapter Three: Looking Ahead

Each day you grow older, I see these wonderful qualities emerging in you:

....

....

....

....

....

....

....

....

An innate talent you possess is: ....

....

....

I hope you inherit my:

....

....

....

....

....

I hope you inherit your father's / mother's (circle one):

....

....

....

....

I hope you inherit your grandmother's:

....

....

....

....

....

....

I hope you inherit your grandfather's:

....

....

....

....

....

....

When you look in the mirror, find at least one positive for every

piece of criticism you give yourself because:

....

....

....

....

....

Always remember that your self-worth should never be based on

how much you weigh because:

....

....

....

....

....

If you ever say something that you regret to someone, you should:

....

....

....

Try to be inclusive in your friendships rather than part of a clique

because: ....

....

....

....

I hope that you help people or contribute to society by: ....

....

....

....

....

....

Some lessons that I have learned about love are: ....

....

....

....

....

A value that I hope to instill in you is:

....

....

....

Always remember that what's on the inside is more important than
what's on the outside because:

....

....

....

I hope you are involved in activities that make you feel good about
yourself because:

....

....

....

....

....

The advantage of maintaining an open mind is:

....

....

Being a respectable woman doesn't necessarily mean: ....

....

....

....

....

Try not to let your body image govern your self-esteem because:

....

....

....

Life lessons that I'd like to pass on to you and your children are:

....

....

....

....

....

....

....

....

I plan to pass this story about our family along to you:

....

....

....

....

....

....

....

....

An important tradition in my family that I hope you continue:

....

....

....

....

....

....

....

....

....

....

My favorite recipe that I want to pass down to you is:

....

....

....

....

....

....

....

....

Take time for yourself to pursue activities that make you feel happy

and fulfilled because: ....

....

....

....

Embrace your femininity but always remember: ....

....

....

....

Some things I have learned from my dearest friends that I want to share with you: ....

....

....

....

....

....

....

....

....

....

I promise to always: ....

....

....

....

....

....

....

....

I promise to never: ....

....

....

....

....

....

Respect for yourself is important because: ....

....

....

....

....

....

Respect for others is important because: ....

....

....

....

....

....

Never forget the importance of having female friendships because:

....

....

....

....

....

....

Be careful of gossip because: ....

....

....

....

....

....

Unselfish support is a significant part of any relationship because:

....

....

....

....

....

....

....

Take people seriously for what they say, feel, and do rather than for how they look because: ....

....

....

....

....

....

The way you conduct yourself around men is a reflection of yourself because: ....

....

....

....

....

Always be courteous to your elders because: ....

....

....

....

....

Acceptance is:

Compassion is:

Serenity is:

Mindfulness is:

One particularly special gift that you have is your ability to:

You should always take the high road and act with integrity because:

....

....

....

....

It's important to always remember that success is a journey, not a destination because:

....

....

....

....

....

Attitude is a little thing that makes a big difference when:

....

....

....

....

....

Surround yourself with the things and people that make you happy and you will find:

....

....

....

....

....

....

Independence is a particularly attractive quality in a woman because:

....

....

....

....

....

....

It's important to always believe in yourself because:

....

....

....

....

....

Solitude is important sometimes because: ....
....
....
....
....
....

Discretion is appropriate when: ....
....
....
....
....

In order to create healthy and enduring relationships:

....
....
....
....
....
....

Jealousy can be toxic to a relationship because: ....
....
....
....
....
....
....
....

Intimacy with your partner is important because: ....
....
....
....
....
....

Performing thoughtful acts for your partner will help keep:

....
....
....
....
....
....

Even if you're deeply in love, relationships can sometimes be:

....

....

....

....

....

When you experience relationship challenges, I suggest:

....

....

....

....

....

....

....

Remember, that in affairs of the heart: ....

....

....

....

....

This is the type of romantic relationship that I hope you have in your life: ....

....

....

....

....

....

....

....

....

....

....

The most valuable advice about married life that I can pass along to you:

....

....

....

....

....

....

....

....

....

The most valuable advice about parent-hood that I can pass along to you is:

....

....

....

....

....

....

....

....

I hope that you will use your talents to:

....

....

....

....

....

....

....

....

It's important for women to stay united because:

....

....

....

....

....

....

In regard to your career, I hope that you will:

....

....

....

....

....

Being a woman in the professional world can sometimes be:

....

....

....

....

Maintaining work / life / motherhood balance can be: ....

....

....

....

....

....

....

....

....

....

It takes much less energy to "live and let live" than harboring

resentments because: ....

....

....

....

....

....

....

....

....

During challenging times in your life, I recommend that you:

....

....

....

....

....

....

....

....

....

An inspirational role model I hope you follow is: ....

....

....

....

It's important to feel good in both body and mind because:

....

....

....

....

....

When you're feeling down:

Just for today, I hope that you:

Laughing with people you love is important because:

A place I love where I would like to take you is:

....

A place I haven't been where I would like to take you is:

....

....

I hope to teach you to be grateful for what you've been given by:

....

....

....

....

....

When you have a difficult decision to make in life:

....

....

....

....

....

....

....

Women often have a thousand things to do, but it's important to always remember: ....

....

....

....

....

....

....

One of the most important things that I believe parents can teach their children is: ....

....

....

....

....

....

....

....

....

....

....

....

I have faith that you will:

....

....

....

....

....

....

....

....

....

As you get older, I am most looking forward to:

....

....

....

....

....

....

....

....

....

Try not to have regrets in life because: ....

....

....

....

....

....

....

....

....

I hope that you remember me after I'm gone by: ....

....

....

....

....

....

....

....

....

....

....

My greatest dreams for you are:

If I could give any gift to you, it would be: ....

....

....

....

....

....

....

....

....

....

....

....

....

....

....

....

....

....

I hope that you celebrate your life by:

The following quote(s) has / have always inspired me, and I hope will inspire you:

In summary, you are the greatest gift of my life because:

....

....

....

....

....

....

....

....

....

....

....

....

....

....

....

....

....

About the Author

Wendy L. Gardner works as a freelance book publicist. She lives in Brooklyn, NY, with her husband, where they continue to learn about the art of parenting on a daily basis from their daughter Willa, as well as their two cats, Poe and E.D.

About the Illustrator

Robert Bretz is an accomplished illustrator and artist who has been creating for more than 20 years. He studied art at the Pennsylvania Academy of Fine Arts, the Philadelphia Museum of Art, and Temple University's Tyler School of Art, where he received his BFA. After a successful career as a commercial art director, he left the corporate world to pursue painting on a full-time basis. Among his work is the highly successful "Simpler Times" series, which has quickly become a favorite among private and corporate collectors worldwide. "Simpler Times" products are now available in boutiques and galleries in the United States and Europe.